On the Other Side of Fifty
&
Rays of Lamentation

Mbu Mbu

Langaa Research & Publishing CIG
Mankon, Bamenda

Publisher
Langaa RPCIG
Langaa Research & Publishing Common Initiative Group
P.O. Box 902 Mankon
Bamenda
North West Region
Cameroon
Langaagrp@gmail.com
www.langaa-rpcig.net

Distributed in and outside N. America by African Books Collective
orders@africanbookscollective.com
www.africanbookcollective.com

ISBN: 9956-790-04-4

DISCLAIMER
All views expressed in this publication are those of the author and do not necessarily reflect the views of Langaa RPCIG.

Table of Contents

Preface

Fifty years of independence and passionate talk of an emerging economy in another thirty-five years: this in brief sums the rhetoric of decolonisation in Cameroon, which the *cinquantennaire* merely glossed over. That in all it may take us eighty-five years to begin the prescribed task of 'emerging' economically, demonstrates the colossal waste that has characterised the passionate discourse of nation-building. Some have referred to what was celebrated in 2011 as 'flag independence' and others as the growth of a banana republic. Whatever the reason for this variation, it attests to the fact that we have managed our country like strangers to a zoo, at once curious at the exotic species and only too eager to walk away with the rarity if the guard is not vigilant enough. Those who gave us a flag also took it as a matter of fact that they gave us our present consciousness. This 'concession' partly explains why their ideological institutions did not accompany them back home. At independence, the return trip for the European was a strategy that fooled and still fools the African, especially through 'civilised' platitudes that make us members of a so-called global family but not participants therein. We have therefore played the blame game for over half a century, and stagnate in the process of accompanying international protocols that still remember when and where to insert the tiny print. We then understand why SAP-arrangements become 'bailouts' in Europe, a process that may make militant postcolonialism a dated concept in the next decade.

Against the generalised backdrop of the postcolonial experience, it is interesting to highlight the uniqueness of every such space. That of Cameroon can become an interesting case study of why a blame culture easily overlaps with efforts to gloss over internal differences. For instance, there is fear in the air, one that is defined by the nurtured hypocrisy of decolonisation, and in which case – we are meant to understand – it is more convenient to talk of English-speaking and French-speaking Cameroonians as patriotic substitutes to Anglophone and Francophone respectively. Unfortunately, this is fear that results from the institutionalisation of new hierarchies in the aftermath of 'independence', the resurrection of autochthonous sentiments as legal tender in the marketing of national unity, and the consequent surrender to the very factors that derail such unity. Stage-managed development becomes a complement to this strategy, and makes strangers of citizens. No authoritative consolation will heal wounds as long as the pretence is not tackled first.

Such alibis constitute the thematic concerns in this volume, even as I concede somehow to formal structure, and will use this as a stepping stone to an explanatory comment. In her very perceptive review of *The Oracle of Tears*, Jennifer Stella makes an important comment that relates to the intersection between the message and the messenger on the one hand and the Self and the Other on the other. Commenting on the poet's expectations of his readers, she 'wonders, then, who his intended audience is; the Cameroonian Diaspora or those who have stayed?' This worry is legitimate only as far as we analyse it within the ambit of colonial education and its celebrated purpose of being able, however dubiously, to measure the IQ of the Other. Characteristic of such education as we see here, is an attempt to split the readership, say Cameroonian, almost condescendingly. On the one hand, the Cameroonian diaspora becomes the privileged authority which can decode every poetic obstacle, while 'those who have stayed' logically scramble around for strands of meaning. Even a casual observer of the two spaces will realise that nothing can be farther from the truth.

No doubt, the writer's meaning is always contested territory beyond authorial confidence. But to tally this into a balkanising sentence that replicates the sequences of 'us' and 'them' even in a borderless world is also to lose sight of how the demise of successive empires is rooted in 'peripheral' energies that must not be taken for granted. But even the indigenous reader can misread the text into vested zones of a cultural anomaly. I remember how, as an undergraduate in the then University of Yaounde, a journalist in the literary column of *Cameroon Tribune* described Bole Butake as an obscene playwright because in *The Rape of Michelle* a police officer asks Mikindong's wife, Akwen, (who had bribed her way to see her detained husband), 'Madam, have you not finished doing it?' Granted that Butake was deliberately suggestive here with regards to how passional equations of national consciousness with ethical illusions expose our cosmetic morality, it is difficult to see how the officer's question adds up to obscenity. In a rare repost, Butake pointed out that only an obscene mind can detect the broth on which it feeds. Such detection is possible even when there is no convincing textual evidence. And that was it, a pedagogical response that was diametrically different from say Bate Besong's almost conceited and anti-establishment posture, wherein he wanted to dictate to the critic how to read his work.

The trajectory is important: our postcolonial condition is still a painful crossroads and still replicates or resists the form of colonial education that makes Samba Diallo, Obi Okonkwo, and Meka interesting intersections in self- or collective-definition. Ironically today, there are still attempts to ensure that both replication and resistance are narrated from the same globalising text; and if one can understand this from a Western lens, it is almost impossible to do so from the African intellectual who endeavours to resurrect Standard English as the ultimate measure of 'civilised' articulation. Our efforts to define ourselves in relative terms has been undermined by a Christian and intellectual conspiracy that ends up talking back *for* the empire. Fortunately, conceptual decolonialists are proving resolute in a philosophical distantiation that makes it necessary to redefine culture without the colossal surrender that intellectual-religious conservatives and fundamentalists foist on us.

This leads me to reflect on another point about the Self and the Other in postcolonial Cameroon; and may begin by asking: what really is postcolonial Cameroon? In Shirley Deane's *Talking Drums* and Richard Bjornson's *The African Quest for Freedom and Identity* we see the type of mediated consciousness that can, and does, threaten a worldview in hardly inadvertent ways, as answer to my query. No doubt Bate Besong asserted rightly that in his research, Bjornson's 'critical excellence would seem to have been diminished by a certain lacunae arising from the non-familiarity or deliberate asphyxiation of works of those new dramatists who in a fleeting moment he refers to as "embattled" West Cameroonians'. To have attempted reading socio-cultural truths from an assumed vantage point betrays a significant degree of inconsistency with the facts at an organic level, and therefore invalidates the whole venture. Both *Talking Drums* and *The African Quest for Freedom and Identity* are instructive texts to the understanding of our space only if we forget for a while that they revive in a significant way the intellectual scars that early European anthropologists imposed on Africana.

Diagnosing the difference in organic terms is the burden of the postcolonial student whether as a diasporic resident alien (to borrow from Gayatri Spivak), or as part of 'those who have stayed' – the need to cry out against the inquisition-type of colonial education that still resurrects its ugly face in the guise of nuancing cultures. New Englishes and its Literatures have come to serve a deserved liberation strategy, which, as I have already suggested, had already been conceptualised as a philosophical momentum to proper decolonisation. Whether it is Kwasi Wiredu, Chinweizu, or Godfrey Tangwa that we are listening to, there is a definite momentum shift in the direction of cultural rehabilitation, and not of assimilation in global flirtation. One may only caution against too much emphasis on an exclusive cultural need that can only degenerate into another form of intellectual idealism, and therefore try to understand why, for instance, Wole Soyinka writes the way he writes, unlike say Chinua Achebe. We can therefore understand why and how as far back as 1934 some Africans were already 'condemned' at birth to see and speak differently, without necessarily violating cultural mores.

A view like this will hopefully make us to adopt a collegiate rather than a hierarchical approach to cultural matters. More specifically, the need to be weaned from a state of what Bob Marley refers to as 'mental slavery' must privilege the raw truth, without varnish, and from which answers must be provided to the deprived constituencies of our socio-cultural space. Such answers cannot always be coated and forced down the throat of the Doubting Thomas of National Unity. As a matter of fact, Thomas is my man among the holy fellows, and in his doubt even of his master's renewed state, I see a challenge to leadership to authenticate itself to the plebe beyond a browbeating affirmation of goodwill and immanence. In the twenty-first century when technological change is altering perceptions in an amazing way, it is a terrible consciousness which still believes that identity cannot be negotiated. Big Brother certainties, if imperative, must also be contextualised.

The Other Side of Fifty is a confession of doubt and fear. But even if such states, the artist is doomed to conjure dawns of optimism after silence of the exhausting voices.

M.T.M,
Ngoaekelle,
11.04.2013

The Beginning

In the beginning
of this nightmare, only
the doubts and the silences after the talks;

the empty spaces in the brain
waiting for meaning
before the curator's worsted memory:

the nagging pulses, rioted loves, gently engaged
à huis clos, and foisted to the weeping horizon
along diplomatic corridors, O Mungo!

Life and death are bred of a shudder, but not
this type, a contrived beginning to end; when the shout
of welcome
echoes the sob of farewell, a new departure.

No More Sirens

Slowly the sirens have died
after town hall rhapsodies
and the rotten tons of miracle speeches.

The sirens are no more
after sounds of dread of doom
and the echo of an emptied millennium.

Alas, the day of prophets, this,
mouthing their flood-smeared sermons,
lisped profanities to a hungry and deaf multitude.

The hour of clemency is past
although heavy flesh still treads the charmed circle
under shaded light, muttering.

And fumbling men of book, exposed, rival
the parroting men of God in soiled cassock
to overtake the requiem hour.

New Dreams

A million dreams have passed over the broken horizon,
a convulsed brow, and a labyrinth of crusted blood,
and abandoned us in a shade of nightmare
with only a staggering faith
in our kindergarten dawn.

Blunted feelers under the aborting sky, we stare
at chalked dreams on arm-boards in silence,
unable to shake off the agonising lethargy,
a storm darkening the horizon already.

The emptied wine gourds
scuttling along stony days and prophesied at shrine of
Tenghehfeng,
only feed a rusted memory. Mopouh of darkly hoods
roars no more in this ruined season of plastic dreams;
the bowels of earth lay unfertilised
and aborted hearts turn away from the lurid sparks
and walk away, heads down.

Generations have been betrayed in this silence of death.

We have watched pregnant seasons in turn
breed speechy monsters on cold, stony paths;
we have been witnesses to Mulafako's grove
denuded at harvest time, in party benevolence;
we have watched his barn of grainy hope
weeviled from roofs-top across the watery border;
we have watched his creek of gushing wells

drained in prodigal platitudes of the speeched monsters,

and still know the fingers that tickle fear
and serve evil on every innocent lintel at Passover,
sterilised fingers that swirl ribbons in kingly heralds
and rub the umbilical stump to numbness.

New dreams then
at the end of the drowse;
new dreams on the dawn of new sleep
to water the sun-parched seed abloom
because the chronicle of purposeless anger
is communal poison; and its acknowledged guilt
salvation of the future.

Toading my Name

Even Master Bull Frog had a vision of the future
mangled in croaky manhood
of the stiffened Eiffel
and the hot air of empty vowels, woven
catchphrase in asphyxia.

But these frenchified delinquents
now straddling the Equator's heartbeat
in *se porte bien* gangsterism,

how they enact a whirlwind in middle of the night,
muting Hiroshima! They shall say,
it was just another case of the naughty
child, refusing to be weaned,
and we didn't take him seriously.

And my name in another burned history hut
defined in Biafra and confirmed in Darfur
at *dodokido* conferences
as remnants of a chaffy memory

but refusing the convenient sentence,
the meanness of brotherhood
so my descendants shall feel the taproot
where they stand.

Anglocam Defined

- *to theoreticians of nationalism*

Anglophone is not a revisable school subject
for despicable exiles of convenience to peddle
across the broken Mungo, a hijacked tale mistold;
but a throb, a yawn, and a smile
that carries decades of faith
against a sinister benevolence.

And Cameroon is not a crucifix of Golgotha
to which we bow in mute supplication
of what is uncreated, a jester's conjuring,
yet made evident at primetime in Mballa Deux;
but a crossroads of disparate multitude
ululating for a dawn and a sensible progeny.

I trail a humble ancestry of stout Fako limbs and
Ndamnyeh frowns
firmed by the horror of my lore, a gift and a hope that
dawn never fails.

When you pass by, in researched and accredited high
sentence,
claiming to define me, don't bare your pale lips for me:
I don't need the flashy smile of hypocrisy,
nor the renewed handshake of eternal slavery: I know
your best
and how can I stoop to such civilized meanness
and the phony knowledge that only brings death?

Like dictionaries and their charted ways,
Versailles painted a bleeding landmark of skulls
and civilised man engraved a status that never was,
a simplistic lore that taught my forebear and me and my
progeny
how not to be membered, conscripted by new slave
masters,
wobbling diplomacy's sneezy
accolades, coyly administered before Weka's nightmare.

But the throb revives in fecund reminiscences
and I feel woven rattle sounds on the evening breeze
and ululate too that dawn, God's undying breath, never
fails.

Hammocks from Bridges

That's the price of a handshake, child,
across the great river
so your children's plenitude should
never forget.

Denuded memory, a patterned selfhood
cloned into Gaullist
cauchemar once upon a grim time, and framed
against the putrid sidewalks

as if there was no beginning
where meaning is
anchored for ritual lore
in your time of need.

Backward trudges with promise to plant
a fig at peak of the Fako, your ritual woe,
my tears revealed and encoded
as evidence of your deprivation.

I enjoin a rascally offspring
with new history books and new beginnings, a
rehabilitated
membrane at bank of the Mungo re-
immersed for robes of manhood, the *jigida* of
womanhood, a tantalising presence at bridgehead
of new encounters from Fako cockpit.

Bamenda

I have walked the crude contours of this town
And step by step covered her blotched lawn.

Her streets, like the churches and schools
Have solemnised every cry, even of fools

Into marshalled tunes of wisdom,
Preaching of dawn's next kingdom.

Martyrs have resurrected from her blooded lanes
Hailing dawn with the passion of puffing danes:

Town of fruitful suffering, land of hope
Tugging leeward the Despot's knotted rope

Because forgiveness your gifted passion
May yet glorify a prideless nation?

Kribi

The new authoritative haven from designer contractors,
millionaires' tryst to customise Ali Baba and a new plenitude
in sodomised tablets of truth, by word of mouth invoked;

the perfumed cabana, whorled in Bikutsi contortions,
a season's greeting card, self-addressed,
with love in pigmy dreams

are just tit-bits of the dittoed elixir,
and who says the God of miracles is dead, when
grunting patriots still conjure a phallic millennium on sand?

Those who have it in surplus also control insurance laws,
scribbled as ideological cacography, and accelerating
the approach to Hades with simmering gospel in lotus dawns.

Ah, grafted place that mocks Victoria's fathomless breakers,
thine is the kingdom now, speculating unknown ways,
my nib's burden to inscribe, and then?

Maroua La Belle

They say, future spot of dreams, pegged
at dawn of the fomenting patriotic passions:

I had imagined Saharan blot on blot unending
where God's tears despise a scrappy lot, neglected;

but the generous heat and precambrian flatness
share a secret and her fructifying abundance weans the
sceptic.

But the Great North Road in Achebean hemispheres
calls forth still,
marker and doom of postcolonial crossroads, our guilt;

how we waste and waste by cheating ourselves in
pretence
after a constituted loot, our national sport,

breeding otherness and the angst of deprivation
to forge opportunistic centres of our imagination,
hollowed;

while Fadimatou, ebony lady in white silks and offering
the future
swirls her braids in winky gests with unheeded prophecy:

extreme weathers have hosted Allah's messengers and
forged a path
with life-giving rod of *nimier*, seeding evergreen eternity

for the native and alien, co-hosts to *my* future without marks
of abuse on the earth where you stand, her beauty to cherish.

When We Sell Cameroon

When we shall have sold this country at last,
and France farts and belches like the man who sold
strictly on cash,
even when her futures on Wall Street
were third grade blood diamonds of an equatorial wail;

When Camdessure's clones, (sneaking in and out of New
York's
five star heavens, and forcing Guinea's exiled laps apart
with threat of dollar power in the scales as lone defence
witness)
affirm the deal's eternal bankruptcy;

the curse shall be ours, makers of the new deal elements
sold at cut-throat prices from Casablanca and New York
while the Menchum breeds waste even this day of
renewed testimonies
at tedious glass palace ritual;

such tons of leprosy consonants
squeezed into the brain, a pre-
cambrian metamorphosis,
another dish of worms on dawn of another beginning:
evil never penalises the innocent;
it returns to the mouth that spewed it,
a recoiling venom whence Moses was nurtured
as Chief Justice of the deprived.

After this ritual of appeasement then,
the story shall be told in endless variations,
how senseful intellectualism helped
derail the dreams of a people in monotonous vistas
of stagnation and endorsed loopholes of Napoleon's
Code as lunar landing for equatorial nightmares in
twenty thirty-five.

The Second Coming

The second coming will never come as preached,
simplistic sequencing of mystery through human
knowledge.

Faked genealogies have constructed a wearisome god
whose omniscience is sustained by intelligent yarns,
the wobbling trinity, the hundred forty-four thousands
hovering the horizon,
and a return that begins and ends in the brain.

God in Eden, after rape of the fruit, suddenly blind
searching for Adam, and no longer omniscient?
Or much later, son as father and the ghostly spirit,
suggesting successorship, son as chopchair then?

Such hindsight evidence, a terrible bore; schemed
parallelism that fits a hypothesis in Roman
metamorphosis.

What Jesus Said

Jesus never said what
they say he said: never
a Christian, he hugged
the scriptures
with faith of the initiate,
burdened with fulfilling his moment,
not eternity.

But those who did not know him
claimed kinship from foisted egos
and edited his utterances into purity
for universal slavery;

and today mankind is bored with monotony,
replicated mindset in hypnosis,
(adjusting to scholars' insights after Galileo),
offering us a collaged saviour always
whose thorned brow
snarls at makers of the eternalising Roman Empire,
his colonisers and usurpers,

like Greece before
and Africa my *africa* after,

while I await an Egyptological find
that should break the chains of spiritual slavery
and spit on patronised translators' versions
of endangered Amharic, after Anta Diop.

Fear of Fire

Slaves of belief, fearing eternal
flames, so we ascertain God
in doubt and falsehood, holy sheep in crass faith.

But what parent with abounding
love, abandons the recalcitrant child
to perdition – mere intimidatory love against dubious
freewill?

Anger so terrible it cannot be assuaged
by child's wail, yet affirms love
and child's heart as password to paradise?

Before the coming of the white man of God
Pa Matiu knew his ritual roots in gifts and cleansing
and yielded to grafting without surrender.

A God of love also understands then
and no wrong, even in aftermath of wronged
father, can resist ritual of supplication.

Jesus My Brother

My strengths and weaknesses
testify to God's image, my original;
but cheerleaders of the diluted liturgy
brand me and offer a whitewashed Christ.

I, God's real photocopy, know
where love and anger converge and mete;
and how to trough this for the better good
remains my burden, falling and rising.

Fifty percent lifestyles I abhor, a sophisticated lie;
for I in God's image, the good the bad the holy,
affirm Jesus my brother, red-mouth carpenter boy,
hijacked
into sheepish manhood by Rome's mulatto brains.

No one owns God, should not appropriate
Himherit, the mystery beyond milky testimonies of
convenience,
and I feel the complex throb and hear God's soft
whisper:
strong-head child of mine, hearken not the conscripting
lot.

Motherly Power
(for Madame Moutou)

Sugar-tongue lady arranging the nation's
purse strings and conjuring Cannan
to weary limbs
from far and near,
chasing files no longer meant to be chased
after my Lord's own promise;

her curses fall
like brimstones, tumbling
from drawn lips,
eyes flashing in twinkling stabs,
because a man of letters
talked like a babe, *merde!*

But she'll roll off
her swivel throne the next second,
a mammy-wagon Diana, digging
into the piled memory of the place
to pacify the naughty child;
and so dies at her load in bits,
day after day, a sheep
with human face

teaching by examples
because nobody
will leave her side
unserved.

Namondo's Garden

She was hired against pundits'
creepy prognostics – remember how the years had
vindicated the chronic sceptics –
the national estate having fed Ali
Baba urchins with two mouths without
oesophagus.

Through sessions of *travaux practique,*
she taught bald heads
with their clumps of darked grey
how not to eat money; instead to
nurse blooms of hope, shoots of the Fako,
in the soul of cut rock.

But she's gone now, a puzzling act of madness,
like the best winds of the knoll
and the weevils begin to sneak back into the ovary,
cunning confederates toasting their bloat
in the littered heart of cut rock.

She had planted her cornerstones of passage here and
there
after half a century's stunted skyline,
but in her sudden aftermath, as converts wept,
names immortalised on marble plaque hail usurpers
of fame unmerited, their rehearsed strategy.

She taught a vainly weaned brood how to say *Mama*
again, but the lactational virus in generic formula

against the nurturing nipple
again targets the young shoots,
the fallowed bloom, and the renewed horizon
and we wonder if God watches the revived rot?

The renaissance had been a shock from foot of the Fako,
Bakingili birth pangs – if you heard the wail – to the
dried womb,
after successive abortions:
then the stooping don sneezed, the wearied student
coughed
as leaves rustled again,
listening to the strange breeze, blinking and repentant.

Painful stirrings of life forgotten I recall:
but the groomed beds for new membrane are withering
already
in a frenzy of infantile cosmetics
seasoned with the yawns and the sighs
when they toast to new year witches.

A Mother's Lament

When she walked in,
unfathomably stiff against those who enslave,
thomases stood up and walked out;

unbelieving naysayers
whose lost faith had bloomed on spiked spaces
of postcolonial aftermaths.

They no longer hope
beyond a New Deal millennia
that serves the same *okro* soup
with a rusted fork
and call it manna.

All they see in an olive halo
is the lightening streak of absolutism
and vow in retreat against
the vampiric babysitters
they have known like sour *okro*.

And there was no Amphitheatre-omniscience
to conjure hindsight soothes, after the hectic days,
now gathered in nostalgic eddies,
the cymballed exeunt.

For Njifor

You hailed me
Across the crossroads
Beyond where we read the stars
Of our becoming.

Iyeuh! Regal flirtations
Humbled rascally strides
With the barbed wire cuts
From cubed cees of the whistling pines:

But now I mourn
The starless sky gaping
On my broken heart
In your sudden departure, without adieu!

Bob, My Man

Bob was a man of knowledge
Unfathomed, it was whispered.

They said he read too much
And suddenly strayed beyond the edge of the world
Where the stars reign.

'You're my only Ni,' he said,
And smiled with a red, bushy mouth;
'I'll wait for you, I will,
When the sun goes home.'

Bob was on his mind all day
As he shuffled paper and scribbled,
A civilised robot, thinking of bills to pay
And rendezvous *not* to miss,
And hurried off at three, for their Obili Carrefour spot.

But a small crowd had gathered there,
Where his man raised his scrap mansion,
To watch the sun rise and go home,
And when he edged his way and asked
They said the man had read too much book
And at last, strayed into the world of his ancestors.

And he turned away, not a tear in his eyes,
And saw the sun straying away from the world,
The eternal companion to the lonely,
The abandoned, seeking rest
Like Bob his man.

Going on Retirement
– for Pa Tamen, Kaytown Boy

He walked in tall and straight,
When the stone buildings stood up
To embrace the Universal Spirit,
For thirsty heart in gown and flat cap.

But now, thirty years gone,
With every secret lodged in his heart,
They ask him to step out on fallen corner-stone
And stepping out, he bows, without his feathered hat.

And who can say, even now,
If valedictions of a cashiered mind
Can revive the juvenescent vow
In new knowledgements of an empty wind?

Of her Laughter

Undulating whiff of incense
in soul-dotting ringlets,
camwood to the gashed day,
mirror against the wrinkled brow…

And there is so much
we take for granted
in a passing ray of life:

like her laughter (and she unknown
to me beyond her sound of music),
the sudden glimpse
into her soul, a universal mate, out there
with friends of uncaring extravagance,
filtering in like divine ripples
through fissures of my dusty cubicle,
Nightingale to a crassly conscious world
to be remembered
only in tears of solidarity which,
the day before,
could have ransomed
all three pegged against the skyline!

Bliss of Innocence

She sucks from her glass of juice
in sharp *pjiu'x* of her age,
believing the woven stories of a past
without storms and a future without
dark clouds; a mental slave
to the arraigned moment after Moses
and ignorant of stem-mother experimentation
with her race, ever blissful
against her stunted age.

After all, it is New Year's eve,
another day of speeches and promises
replicating the served drudgery during which,
unknown to her green appetite,
(as she licks her fingers and sucks her straw)
her womb was auctioned to
Europe's united nations chieftain for a feast of adorned
hollowness, the dishes and bottles
patented to a dubious nutritionist
dabbling in test-tube miracles
in a no-go zone of the Elysée.

After Purupa*-in-Picasso
(for Dr Kinni Nsom)

Visages of the past,
dotted on polished floor
and on painted walls,

offering a broken smile
resurrected on splashed canvass
through the scars of time
in museum-trek.

Those who *know* are
tickled, and laugh with
nurtured feeling, recognised,

and dream of new bridges
to ferry the woes of man
back into the bosom of the past, reborn.

Those stumps long neglected
issue with new breath
and assert the picture framed
from fallen arms, fingers, or toes
or even a broken lip;
and from the chips of neglect
restore the sympathy of soft dreams onto stiff lids.

---

* traditional artist and gunsmith in Pinyin

Oh, pristine Gatherer fed with
legendary patience,
saving those archaeological pieces
of a wild jungle tooth or the broken bellows
or other such mirages confluenced on
tattered jute or canvass:

America will rush here
in the dawn of your incarnation
to be born again
refreshed from her toxic
loves and chores, sneezing.

She will find herself again
in fear and in love,
frightened in the discovery
of things long forgotten,
the mystery of the cycle
coming back from across the Atlantic
in ritual knowledge,
a new grain for new sheaves
from your Spring womb.

Soul Unloved

My life is a toy
a marked thing of black
and white stripes for beauty;
toyed about by the select watchers
of this land, who awaited me
nude in shamelessness,
on my meekly creeping from
the warm, dark world, into this cold womb.

They are the finders, also the finders,
of a Cause, who toy the place
this way and that way,
on a swollen prophecy;

against my life of feared heresy, and
march the marble in *ideologized* swings.

So I dangle from
doll-pegs of the show
like a misery, waiting
in my comfort, on
the winds of their desire.

Ashes

Cripple me now, if you must:
As your Gods of blood will,
Strike me now in camouflage of will.
So maim me fast, unbudded,
Maim me before my hour, when
My blood may corrupt your dish.
Then let me lurch in the green shade of the petal;
Let me hobble in the momentary lulls of withered pain;
Let me lie then, in the shadow of my immolation,
And contemplate the moment of the Mystery.

The Release

There's liberation in forgetting,
the heart no longer mangled by
tethering dreams.

Crucifix of Miss Havisham's void
in equatorial lush, my portion,
and the dangling noose and a tiny worm wriggling.

Passion is but a whim
nurtured into eternal vines, discarded,
to seek one's soul where it waits;

pleasing flight of my nativity, this,
to the doorsteps of dawn
and a nurturing cry?

A While Ago

A while ago now seems a generation
During which hoodlums usurped the market square and
Managed aggregates of smile,
Navigating Guernica in psalmist solemnity.

Epicurean decades easily collapse into a strangled
Nightmare and phantom patriots
Gather around the corpse of the nation
In self-vindication of what was never done.

We'll auction the future to a French tick
And think paradise is ours forever,
When forever is now just a while ago,
The sickening sensation of birthed rot.

Beads of Flame

Beads of flame skirt
artesian dreams
under nebulous sky
when volleyed contentment
rolls on the laps of siren glee.

But a slash of cunning,
sudden at skygates,
heralds a prophet's apparition
and everywhere streams of tears
cart constipative sins
into the hollow chambers of History.

Beads of flame,
God's redemptive crackers,
must shower sulphous hearts
like resurrecting winds
along funereal footpaths ...

Lonely Migrant

At crossroads of heart,
Quartered, the lonely migrant
Meditative but uncertain.

Generous flash of teeth from
Marauders of the guarded ovary
Across bumps,
Instantaneous and fixed
Axing the cord that feeds the heart.

Not now the moment of luxurious pauses
Nor recognition of amends
When the water breaks and a new cry
Echoes a world that was made docile by lip-service
And a footnote from grumpy Paris.

Untrimmed Christ was a lone voice
Rubbed in the mud of his fame;
And here on the nurturing banks of the Mungo
A Fako shoot shall save the day.

Pilgrim

Open spaces for blind steps
and another blunder along the muddy track
after mirages
coiling ever ahead
in the aftermath of repeated blunders;

with a ripped heart
begging for the stars and a rose, and wondering
about a promised dawn
and a peace of mind…

The fresh cuts on weak flesh,
my awkward penance after failure to cry foul
in the ruined paradise

as builders of the nation, always a-building,
giggle at lunchtime, experimenting
their chopsticks from Beijing, a staggering
partnership from start, when the nation is auctioned
anew
for an emerging halo
in *hing-hong* rubbish because one must be careful these
days.

Bondage

-Sunday, on campus

Certain tendencies enslave the mind
Like love in picturesque seasons,
Or devotion to tasks of days, as to the Lord,
Before *de luxe* whirlwinds sneer at menial fingernails.

Oh, these whispers, through
Chinks of heart, riddled by desire:
Blight my day, if nothing else,
Before I dream again
Of new airs.

Roulette dreams sink mines, fathomless
And fertile,
Into sniggering brains
Railing the sidewalks with mangled love
On second-hand tiers, tick-tack, tick-tack,
Toward Avenue Kennedy's Derby.

This desire, inscrutable and as dear,
Must shore my woes, troughed at floodgates
Of knowledge,
When in my heavy heart lyrical days
Still tangle resolve, with tears and blossoms,
And seed habitual lusts
For back glances of condescension.

This desire, inscrutably dear, tears the heart asunder,
And surrenders to stubborn clock-whispers on the wall

Before resurrection at wreath time, of memories
Dear and gone, on tablets,
In absurd collectors' chambers.

Beyond Caring
-Yaounde-Douala highway

Now I think of death —
when it shall come,
if it must, just as it shall:
of the falling stairs of darkness in swift flight
across horizons of oblivion, falling, ever falling,
when worldly cares in surge
shall resurrect over new dawns.

This snaking track, gliding
beneath my soul of its own will, gliding,
leads to death, when on the last stair
of the falling dream, falling,
I shall worry no more.

Death comes like a sigh
in sweet repose
if days unschemed you'd hailed,
serving god in man without
congregated wantonness and flourish;

but like a chronic thing
he wastes his victim into a sty-like
hallucination, through passages of hell,
serving god on the dry tongue
of estranged fanfare, wasting.

So my thoughts of now, as of the end,
recuperate on distance-covered
and passing space, philosopher

to myself, my own medic
and redeemer, waiting for the hour
unknown.

When I Fall

I have always thought my days
numbered in pious anxiety
to reach God;

to know the unknown paths of purity
and walk in the humble acclamation
of submission.

But they say, he's a Christ-hater, the way he talks,
a branded triple six lout, spitting rot.

Every second seemed my last, clad in a sudden
stalemate of indecision, when like
a glittering balloon, all my hope kisses a blade!

This thought has disturbed me,
challenged my steps,
and tripped, unable to stand,
I fell.

Mourners

They come like they'd love to leave, rushing,
And weep like strangers to the truth, lying:

They conjure castles of pity
And restore wreckages of mirth

To a life-hungry multitude
Hoping never to die.

Epigraph

For those who shall sing my eulogy,
Paint not a single word unmeant
Nor chant the sweetest verse undeserved,
And the bitterest phrase with frankness

Else I shall groan in my castle of mud
And sweet repose withered
By unfair parchments of living fear,
From wilting tongues of hasty lust.

For it seems I shall not see my flower bloom
Nor breathe of her fragrance when I fly
And fly, over the sickled hills of pains and sorrows,
Into my apportioned valley of forgetfulness.

Waiting

(Lazare concerto on broken strings of the Nation)

-i-

I rushed here
at early dawn, heavy
at heart and seeking a god,
a sleekly-worded petition in folder under armpit.
Every passing hour heaved a
heavy sigh in rheumatic impatience.
Boisterous men with identical outfit breezed in,
at regular intervals, such
well-fed chaps, puffing Party epithets
against forehead embraces like bulls,
their swollen trunks as proof,
and threw a distant glance
at the line of waiters, such ideological nuisance,
before punching at the guarded door of authority.
They possess the key to heaven in kin-celebrity,
someone whispered, if only
to divert lurking desperation.

Speechlessness at such patriotic
moments becomes a pal
and lost in her sullen confines
one is blessed with courage
to forget so much and run away
from oneself, behind closed lids.

So we wait for the endless
in-and-out abuse of power,
wishing God will not come too soon

and catch us off-guard.

Watery eyes and yawning mouths
know the wait too and testify,
in silent phases: it is despotic
to force a will, to try to cripple it,
so why try to stifle the yawn
coming when it must,
simply because the weary neighbours
stare at you, hungry for a promise,
and you wish you were a gentleman,
one of the ogre-eye visionaries!

-ii-

They begin to disperse in silent farewells,
the waiters, muted masks: just look and understand,
if you must, but seek not to know
too much of their sneaky destinations;
the roads to heaven are many
and many are they who'll never
see God, huddled on their heavy thighs, waiting.

But we linger awhile, after announced arrival of grey-
haired
town-crier, mouthpiece of broken vision
at the National station; he had rallied a nation's ire
that Saturday afternoon in May,
staged tongue against tongue across the river
and tickled a region against itself, as grease
to the Emperor's emergent cunning,
after which Dimabola lead-singers besieged the streets.
The few and fewer who still dare believe in God's time

as reprieve in after-work trysts,
and yet groan over schemed shame
of waiting with long stiff faces;
they espy through crack of opening
door to squeeze in swaggering Mouthpiece, a rare
glimpse of earthly paradise
as man puts on God's own cloak
and sways on the throne of authority, puffing.

The bell rings again as before and again the waiters
jump with crackling joints
and hopeful hearts.
Then the secretary goes in and then out,
signals a second secretary
who signals the third *to report*, in and then out.
Then glasses clink on a silver tray
and soon, from the half-opening
door to flush out the secretary,
puffs of canned imports
announce the hour of the miracle:
the recently admitted, carrying
heaped buttocks, are God's own
chosen few who in their seats
of stuffed cotton, overwhelm paradise.

How long can the longing heart wait then
for the expected glories of heaven
with cracked, smiling lips
because the good slave never complains?
Anger is a cunning thief when
man is ridiculed into a pauper
at the gates of ostentation,

begging for admittance.
Man curses God in deprived moments
while in and out the recognised few
come and go, tickled into guffaw
by feasting and solution, singing
God's glories in filial sonorities.
So we wait, starved supplicants
without the will pray anymore.
God is deaf, he is not for the meek
and faithful anymore, barred from us
by tribal swagger in ideological stew…

Still we wait, now a straggling few,
happy in the delusion
that in the Lord's Kingdom
there is space for all.

-iii-
I don't aspire for the daisy throne
of feathered acclaim under neon skies;
I cuddle my hope, waiting
for my bamboo stool on dusty spot
in God's allotted space
where the earth never lies.
What does it matter where I lie
as long as it affords me a glimpse
of the haloed Presence, why
should it matter?

(And the voice within me, saying:
rebels are not born, no;
wooden gods breed them

at fibrous end of communal cord)

Even as entrails of the recent feast
are carted off and the stench
of heaven infects weary nostrils
and rings of sneezes hypnotise
the divine atmosphere, and as the
appointed god remains supreme
and enclaved from prodigal lusts,
what does it matter, and why?

-iv-

Blinded by the guile of man
for man, I say 'No!
God is not for me, perhaps
never was, and I'll seek him
no more, if I must stay out of paradise,
no more a-waiting, no more a-stooping to conquer'.

On a sudden impulse,
I kick the straying crumbs of paradise
off my heavy feet,
blistered by too much hope in waiting.
Seems the hands of God stretch
only to those who punch
at his gate with gold, printless thumbs;
those who must squat at gastronomic rituals
to lick his boots in belching Passovers,
but not me, rising to follow
the stretched day, king to my heart
and seek out gutter philosophers,
such truth-peddlers who scratch beneath the whitewash.

From ante-chamber of à huis-clos
whispers in continuum, of nation-building
and patriotism and party discipline and
hero worship, etcetera
etcetera, nothing garnered
except the eternal pain with no diagnosis;
nothing for posterity because pot-breakers
may testify to God's will.

In retreat, I talk to myself and wish for the little things
that others neglect:
the sigh for instance, when a drop of joy
favours my bowl.

My tongue is clumsy
against the sleek Larousse vowels,
and I stumble in explanation, excusing
myself for no crime committed, at the gate.

Those watery eyes
strained in use and abuse,
wasted by too much expectation;
and the nostalgia for things
never known because pigs have more dignity
than horses, brother;
and suddenly, misery
hurls my cup of gall
down my throat, a terrible shudder.

I squint for the stars
and for the moon, born again,
over the cactus horizon;

I summon Ngariba† might
to stay awake, and sane
but the winds pull me into pirate ways
and I fall, foaming.

Others know their pace
in fine measure
and strive without fear
or effort toward their
dripping summits,
and gather baskets replenished
by mere desire.

The trickle down my brow,
and into snarling lips, so salty to the tongue,
consoles the drooping day too,
with the cord slipping out of grip
with a jazzy sigh...

And at flashing point of dark horizon
when madness saturates the soul
and conquers a rational thought:
my mind is crazed
over shadows of
desire: the many things
I seek and sacrifice
myself for, quester for a dream;

how do I subdue the daemon
in me screaming for deliverance

---

† legendary village fighter

and fulfilment, against a lie?

The day of heroism is over
for me as patriots pack bag searching for colours
on new horizon, but my tale is still
untold, wrapped in withering thoughts
and whispered in dangling phrases, like these, in my soul;
bystanders in evening wear and watching the blot,
gape at my exposed breast,
and trail a *quartier* rumour or two
before scurrying off
after their bottles and *mini-mino* dreams.

Appointments and Installations
for JM Essomba, Pr.

Glints of hypocrisy
tumbling from dental fractures;
hour of the blessed,
their eternity to fête
in the groomed aftermaths!

Brazen eulogists from fattening sties
roll honeyed tablets with crusted tongue-tips
to a dulled multitude.

People who will toast to see you crawl, suddenly
broker testimonies from invisible scrolls,
negotiate your landing on the sun with no Pathfinder,
and testify to your Christhood.

Black Samaritan, you, they insist, weaned
instantly, from their nostalgic valves
of alma mater kinships,
even collegial gimmickry with guffaw:

Old pilots with God-dream to en-
law heredity in high office
when they drop, or get dropped
at last, a sallow paleness as of bloated pigs
in three-piece manacles, how they
vow eons of milk at Edensgate!

Withering seasons too have their term
when *asamba* masquerades bleed the parched earth
with rattling retribution, pigeonhole
prodigal rascals with growth from French vines
into crack-brain clinics
so they can learn how to live, at last.

If Anomah Ngu Were No Anglofool

State coffers would have been rallied
to hail his hypothesis;
he would have known that the greatest patriot
is a looter and doublespeaker even of the Queen's
tongue.

Ibadan had blessed a miracle but the milk of
fatherland got into his head and his restive steps
would not rest until gurgling Matajem
consoled his wearied manhood, a humble returnee.

Ah, the allure of statesmanship and the exposure,
slave to the Nation, servant to the guttered constituents,
but ridiculed by a charlatan peer whose only merit
is alleluia pedagogy, patronised, at the Hilton.

Anglofools have licked their wounds
in this Union, pretending to a brotherhood of interest,
but only a colonialist scam, and watch the senseful chaps
build the nation as private booty, denying the future.

Se Porte Bienhood

Against stranglehold of
pollsters and spin-doctors
the whistle-blower had sniffed
the spice of tabloids;

his tale of why dreams are deferred
sharpened the syringes of hired Squealers
who inoculate the public
conscience as Big Bro standard-bearers
with sleek motions of support, thereafter;

their shades of insanity are hailed as
refractions of Pilate's wisdom,
fence-sitters' ruse before the pause
by the banks of swollen Mungo, humming.

Okonkwo's Sword

Masculine streaks of salty sweat
cut across the furrowed countenance
to announce a cavalry
in shrieks of doom;

unsheathed slash of manhood
against glint of stubborn helmets,
to forfeit a shameful pedigree;

but into the opening
decades, gaping
Ikemefuna mouths
soundlessly wait for water.

World conferences in cyber space
Listen to Bob
Geldorf
Dylan
Marley
and sigh like aftermath of a dot-com bubble
hailing Wall Street's one percent
like the sneeze from Harare,
when Dinard snarls-in-Popoli
convulse the lily horizon.

Chopstick Diplomacy

Such dragon embraces
of a postcolonial scam that insult
the memory of a people under twenty-first century noon,
and our leaders soiling their sleek, designer lapels
at staged photo show of Beijing's epicurean farce;
backward pedagogy and the glee
of new imperialism, our woe. We've survived, you may say,
on American crumbs from gilded table of the lucky
one percent in Wall Street paradise, but Beijing
preys even on the maggots from our pit latrines,
and shocks legendary Parisian greed for equatorial teats.

What blindness drags us along China's blood-builded Wall then,
when her Old Guards rehearse Wall Street
superlatives but not as Democrat or Capitalist?
Confused Politburo landlords, seeding confusion into new enclaves,
and ours a juicy chunk, blind to imminent Beijing Bubble
because China's new taste buds are conceptualised at Cambridge,
designed by General Motors, and served
in Disneyland elixir with reeded Coke at the manager's Easter discount.

Tiananmen Square was a nursery, Beijing's
dread and lie, and every tropical dictator's April fool,

when the whitewash cannot fool her formatted billions
forever,
because the Tank Man, O lone Warrior against the
billion Red Guards,
dared the bloody bluff like a Robin Hood shoot
sprouting
on Nottingham campuses in Chinaland.

We don't need Beijing's weevilled goodwill,
her doomed messianism not defined,
a forgery of ideology forging newer chains
and the prospection of blood and more blood
after Gorbachev's feelers, ridiculed.
Castro tried but failed to conjure eternity in the shadow
of a sickle and hammer,
because self-interest, even poorly nurtured, overwrites
glossy communal overtures patterned as brain-drilled
testaments of good faith for a neutered humanity;
so this hybrid pedagogy in political science
from Beijing's coney-eyed pedagogues
makes me sick with funereal
prophecy in 2035.

A Jawbone

Give me a jawbone,
O God, a jawbone wrath;
this misery,
fed by decades of wait and hope,
is a mockery of the sun and the moon,
and yet the plebe laughs because

he cannot cry. A jaw-
bone, God, hear this one last time,
and I will have my peace
after the silence of the fattened lie.

Plaintiff Call

Webs of calvary greetings scrawled
across the heavy skies; frantic
intimations of the heart
from exile waves, returning ...

I hear your plaintiff whispers
seeking solace in faery hope;
I hear your wails too
seeking anchor on sandy shores ...

And I, who have known such sounds before,
and cuddled the whispers and the wails in night tunes;
I, who bore the stab in ventricle chambers
and the stifled crimson yawn:

Sudden prospects, denied,
proclaim interred glory
with the revelations of the void.

So I hear your whisper, and know what
negligent acrimony insinuates
your doomed fall, wailing.

The orphaned soul is wisest,
suckled in the lapse of glory
over hollowed balm of memory.

The Dying Heritage

In the name of Jesus, we shout, parroting
what is parroted; in the mighty
name of Jesus, we bow finally,
not hearing in our new voices
the swansong of African heritage because
the universal ancestor, uprooted from his patch,
is balm to scars of savagery.

Duplicities of power have arraigned
indigenous energy,
shackled the God we feel
for an erected Roman concept in the brain
strategically defined and redefined over time;

and God weeps again
to see us so sheepish

abandoning our path to the shrine
for lily verbs and milky metaphors
whose constructed God has dashes
and makes the world a weeping arena.

Unoka's Flute

In the midst of the orchestrated decay, and the
hilarious acclamations from dentured
lips on TV swearing to God
the father the son the holy ghost,
a broken amen;

where is the bard and the soothing
lyric? Where the balm of Gilead after
the Madiba? Only a hoarse voice
in the grip of patronage and rejecting
their own militant cries for salvation because looted
paradise is here on earth?
Harlequins of a nightmare at noon,
their convenient narratives as pseudo-
deconstructionists of the colonial sentence
mimicking what they adore to hate,
mere intellectual orgasm, and the shame of it,
awaiting their inheritance in the constructed paradise,
a postcolonial gimmick?

Sodden (wo)manhood in this graveyard quietude
in which even God is bought and sold in devalued
silver of a French stock crash
revives our hate and the love of it: high profile
sons of the land, by-products of colonial garbage
their certified credentials prophesying doom
because the bard was not man enough to win the day:
how do we retrieve the flute
from the Evil Forest and revive the wilting day?

Apocalypse

Beads of flame skirt
artesian dreams
under nebulous sky
when volleyed contentment
rolls on the laps of siren glee.

But a slash of cunning,
sudden at skygates,
heralds a prophet's apparition
and everywhere streams of tears
cart contemplative sins
into the hollow chambers of History.

Beads of flame,
God's redemptive crackers,
must shower sulphurs hearts
like resurrecting winds
along funereal footpaths ...

Reddening Skyline

My looted conscience
sings a frontier song
(and they stare at me)

amidst tombstones of wilted hope, despicable,
yet consoling to my wounded name
(and I feel alleluia in my bones).

Resolutions adjourned every New Year's Eve,
such diluted yarns with me a contingent
species for collateral toasts; and anniversary bouquets
drip tears of my progeny:

we have listened
to the alibis that camouflage
failed promises on Darwin's paradise
with no state of the union lullaby for recompense
even as slashes mark the skyline
easterly of rumbling Fako;

and know better now
how not to hope from a hope-bereft
lineage serving vinegar at teatime.

The Piss of Peace

When campaigners for world peace
from Tsinga's knoll
sermonise on Time Heals All
to the jazz of Dimabola lead-singers
and drag me
and my ancestors,
me and my progeny
into the hall of dripping mouths,
they forget how the mirrors of Versailles
raised and then humbled the Kaiser,
his Pilot that was, and the crown of shame enticed.

For there is peace that mocks the gauze,
its spectral grin a pain;
shatters the dreams it weaves,
and laughs Dracula balms of love
across the monumental waterway:
and how can I abide
only to slip in the peace of
overfed patriotism?

Blinking Horizon

I wish for the little things
that others neglect:
the sigh when a drop of joy
favours
my bowl.

Those watery eyes
strained in use and abuse,
wasted by too much expectation;
and the nostalgia for things
never known,
and suddenly, misery
hurls my cup of gall
down my throat.

I squint for the stars
and for the moon
over the cactus horizon;
I summon Gibraltar might
to stay sane, and awake
but the winds pull
me into pirate ways
and I fall, foaming.

Others know their pace
in fine measure
and strive without fear
or effort toward their
dripping summits,

and gather baskets replenished
by mere desire.

The trickle down my brow,
and into snarling lips
salty to the tongue,
consoles the sterile day too,
with the cord slipping out of grip
with a sigh...

Courtship of the Pistol

Ibsen's Delilah was a confused Mammy-Wata
whose bosom recoiled from Oriental spices
even   as   she   simmered   within   against   Kipling's
extravagance.
Sir Punch had draped her in unearthly ribbons
and cautioned her against exotic fruits of the Congo.
After all, a Pole had negotiated Englishness
into canonical faith, whose inroads
like allures of the Atlantis, replicated
professed certainties beyond the Sahara.

Time passed and passed, constituencies changed
but the new landlords with Negroid energies
kissed the pistol and devised three-piece gunocracies
that became the envy of Napoleon Bonaparte
whose provincialism had amazed
snoring monarchies into renewed scheming at Waterloo.

Today then, after Nkrumah and Mazrui,
three-piece gunocrats on Sphinx's third leg
still legitimise eternity at statehouse, buoyed
by   snivelling   book   surgeons   pretending   as   Ogun
disciples,
whose only merit is a parroting ability
at crumbs time, always footnoting
Kipling's forebear because there must be a reason
why we are so disgusting;

and vow through published data, how
Sankara and Rawlings were such fools,
Anan a bigger fool, and Madiba the biggest of fools,
who invested ludicrous strategies,
confused mendicants at a game of interest,
and why doubt then why we are so disgusting!

The Exile

He is never born; he is
made and groomed on home turf into dispirit
by men of God insulting
God; by men of book
insulting Theory; and dramatising
a yarn they doubt just because
the sane must be transformed into Chichidodos
to vindicate the theorised muddle:

the preacher and the intellectual have failed us,
created invisibilities that preach eternity and light
at end of virtual tunnel; and cushioned
the schemed and rehearsed truancy
in enclaves of deprivation:

so these invisible tears
are salvation for my children
born to inherit the nightmare I fed.

Jeremiah's Tears

Even when we heard it before,
the green veldt that succumbed to a rapist's tactics,
like nomads' tales retold in transition
but always toward the beckoning horizon;

even when ocular proof confounded us into a sickening
shudder
after cobwebbed portals of Buea
and the gawky cliffs of Abakwa Golgotha, signposted
by my forebear as annals to tomorrow:

how come we still believe
such doomsday emissaries whose rally point
is a doomed sigh along broken tracks,
under sunken roofs, a deserted market place?

My eyes have witnessed desecration of the shrine
while hired fingers seek the taproot beneath the Fako,
hoping too to change the course of the River
beyond which we shall weep no more: unblinking eyes
and as tearless, firmed by the endurance of wrong,
how else can they celebrate myself
except by sniffing new airs, a new day?

How not to Define Patriotism

After watching a jingoistic eunuch, hero-worshipping a
lie,
the bits of over-chewed *goro*
splashed in bland tele-grin on infamy,
such national currency in Party fanfare
that replants the crucifix of Marley;

Oh, such collateral pleasantries stewed as
patriotic lotto for a few – how they
have dwarfed my days of hope for this triangle,
sanctioned
rot as rarefied speak for national colours in tatters
and approved cut-and-past testimonies

even as I rally for stride away for a root and voice, back
across the ridiculous hammock, back
to the beginning of recorded time where the fight was
always with elbows,
and back, yes, to the tablet beneath the Rock,
to pronounce my age.

The Other Side of Gold

Distance, tamed by the fossils of your infallible brain
has planted question marks on my tongue.

On the other side of fifty, *jabvou* or genuine,
after the ludicrous ads in confetti
at prime time, to pacify De Gaulle's ghost and progeny;
and after the groan of joy, our cosmetic art,
I still remember the greenery of Weka's backyard
when the palace gong heaved a rhythm of dawn:

but now, in the sudden harmattan of your frenzy,
locusts in a season of plenty
and with every fact twis-
ted and twi-
sted again and again, twine in a land of locust,
I count endless question marks,
heavy as a fiftieth milestone, on my tongue.